Book 2

Literature & Comprehension

Writing Skills

Language Arts

Assessments

K12®

Book Staff and Contributors

Beth Zemble   *Director, Alternative Learning Strategies; Director, English Language Arts*
Marianne Murphy   *Senior Content Specialist*
Amy Rauen   *Senior Instructional Designer*
Mariana Holliday, David Shireman   *Instructional Designers*
Mary Beck Desmond   *Senior Text Editor*
Suzanne Montazer   *Creative Director, Print and ePublishing*
Jayoung Cho   *Senior Print Visual Designer*
Stephanie Shaw Williams   *Cover Designer*
Karen Draper   *Senior Manager, Assessment and Research*
Barbara Allen   *Assessment Developer, Reading*
Nancy Freedman   *Assessment Specialist*
Tim Mansfield, Lisa Moran   *Writers*
Amy Eward   *Senior Manager, Writers*
Susan Raley   *Senior Manager, Editors*
Alden Davidson   *Senior Project Manager*
David Johnson   *Director, Program Management Grades K–8*

Maria Szalay   *Executive Vice President, Product Development*
John Holdren   *Senior Vice President, Content and Curriculum*
David Pelizzari   *Vice President, K¹² Content*
Kim Barcas   *Vice President, Creative*
Laura Seuschek   *Vice President, Assessment and Research*
Christopher Frescholtz   *Senior Director, Program Management*

Lisa Dimaio Iekel   *Director, Print Production and Manufacturing*
Ray Traugott   *Production Manager*

Illustrations Credits

All illustrations © K12 unless otherwise noted

About K12 Inc.

K12 Inc., a technology-based education company, is the nation's leading provider of proprietary curriculum and online education programs to students in grades K–12. K^{12} provides its curriculum and academic services to online schools, traditional classrooms, blended school programs, and directly to families. K12 Inc. also operates the K^{12} International Academy, an accredited, diploma-granting online private school serving students worldwide. K^{12}'s mission is to provide any child the curriculum and tools to maximize success in life, regardless of geographic, financial, or demographic circumstances. K12 Inc. is accredited by CITA. More information can be found at www.K12.com.

978-1-60153-304-3

Printed by Action Printing, Fond du Lac, WI, USA, April 2017

Contents

Literature & Comprehension

Unit Checkpoint Learning Coach Instructions
Critical Skills Practice 4

Explain to students that they are going to show what they have learned about reading and answering questions about nonfiction passages, directions, and fiction passages, and about summarizing a fiction passage.

1. Give students the Unit Checkpoint pages.

2. Read the directions together.

3. Use the Answer Key to score the Checkpoint, and then enter the results online.

4. Review each exercise with students. Work with students to correct any exercise that they missed.

Part 1: Nonfiction Passage

Have students read "A Town Like No Other" and answer the questions.

Part 2: Directions

Have students read the recipe and answer the questions.

Part 3: Fiction Passage

Have students read "Sandy's Share" and answer the questions.

Part 4: Summarize a Fiction Passage

Have students write a summary of "Sandy's Share."

Unit Checkpoint
Critical Skills Practice 4

Part 1. Nonfiction Passage
Read the passage and answer the questions.

The town of Vail, Colorado, was founded in 1966.

A Town Like No Other

1   Colorado is a state that most skiers love, and it is easy to see why. The Rocky Mountains climb high into the sky. There's plenty of snow, and there are hundreds of ski towns to visit. Yet one Colorado town stands out from all others. No ski town in the state is better than Vail.

2   The best word to describe many ski towns in Colorado is *stuffy*. Some might say *snobby*. In

some ski towns, people care about the skiers' clothes or how new their skis are. Vail is not like that.

3   Vail is a place for everyone. No one judges others in Vail. The people are **affable** and open and always looking to meet new friends. They do not care what others look like or how they dress. People in Vail don't care if your skis are old or new. They just want everyone to have fun. In fact, people in Vail are too busy enjoying themselves to look down on others.

4   Of course, not every other ski town is full of snobs. There are nice people everywhere. There are people in other ski towns who love it when visitors of all types come to enjoy themselves. But there aren't enough of these friendly folks. There are just too many people who seem to want to have Colorado all to themselves and their snooty friends.

5   At first glance, all of the ski towns in Colorado can seem alike. They are all beautiful. They all offer lots of fun and excitement. Yet only one town is sure to give all visitors a warm welcome. Only one town is a home away from home for everyone who comes there. That town is Vail, the greatest little ski town there is.

1. Which sentence shows the author's opinion?
   A. All ski towns are exactly alike in every way.
   B. Vail is the best ski town in Colorado.
   C. Vail is one ski town that is full of snobs.
   D. All ski towns are totally different.

2. How does the author try to influence how readers feel about ski towns other than Vail?
   A. The author says that everyone in Vail cares how much another person's clothes cost.
   B. The author says that other ski towns have many nice restaurants.
   C. The author uses words like *stuffy* and *snobby* to describe other ski towns.
   D. The author points out how far away other ski towns are from Vail.

3. Which best restates the main idea of Paragraph 3?
   A. Vail residents always use old skis.
   B. The cost of clothes matters a lot in Vail.
   C. People in Vail are quite busy.
   D. Everyone is accepted in Vail.

4. Based on context clues, what does the word *affable* mean in Paragraph 3?
   A. friendly   B. mean   C. tall   D. busy

5. How do readers know when Vail was founded?
   A. The title tells them.
   B. The first paragraph tells them.
   C. The picture caption tells them.
   D. The conclusion tells them.

Part 2. Directions
Read the recipe and answer the questions.

Breakfast Pie

Make breakfast for the whole family with this simple recipe.

Ingredients
- 1 frozen pie crust
- 3 eggs
- 1/3 cup of milk
- 6 slices of cheese
- 1 pound of chopped spinach

Preparation
Place pie crust nearby on the counter.

Steps
1. With the help of an adult, preheat the oven to 375 degrees.
2. Crack the eggs into a large bowl.
3. Use a fork to whip the eggs.
4. Add milk to the eggs and stir.
5. Add spinach to the egg-milk mixture.
6. Lay the slices of cheese over the bottom of the pie crust.
7. Fill the pie crust with the egg-milk-spinach mixture.
8. With the help of an adult, place the pie on a rack set in the middle of the oven. Bake for 35–40 minutes.
9. With the help of an adult, remove the pie from the oven. Turn off the oven. Allow pie to cool for 5–10 minutes.

LITERATURE & COMPREHENSION

Name _____ Date _____

6. Based on the drawing, how should the cheese slices look on the bottom of the pie crust?

   A. They should lie in an even layer.

   B. They should all sit in pile in the middle.

   C. They should all be pushed to one side.

   D. They should be along the outer edge of the crust only.

7. When should spinach be added when making this dish?

   A. before cracking the eggs

   B. after adding milk to the eggs

   C. after removing the pie from the oven

   D. before whipping the eggs with a fork

8. Which step should be done first when making this dish?

   A. Add cheese to the pie crust.

   B. Place the pie crust in the oven.

   C. Turn off the oven.

   D. Preheat the oven.

9. Which would be the best way to learn how to make another kind of pie?

   A. Follow this recipe but use different ingredients.

   B. Find and follow a different pie recipe.

   C. Read a story about someone who makes pie.

   D. Read an article about the history of pie.

10. What would happen if Step 8 was done before Step 7?

    A. The cheese would not melt in the pie crust.

    B. The eggs would never get whipped.

    C. The egg-milk-spinach mixture would not cook.

    D. The oven would never be turned off.

Part 3. Fiction Passage
Read the passage and answer the questions.

Sandy's Share

1   It was only ten in the morning, but the day was already a hot one. Max took a sip of water. Then he placed the glass back on the small table on the sidewalk in front of his house. He stood and admired his work for a moment.

2   On the table sat 20 or 30 stones that Max had polished with his rock tumbler. There were stones of red, white, green, and brown. There were big stones and small ones. They sparkled in the morning sunlight.

3   Max smiled as he looked at the stones. It had taken him days to collect them all and days more to polish them. Now he was about to be rewarded for his hard work. He took another sip of water and cleared his throat.

4   "Rocks!" Max called out. "Get your finely polished rocks! They're just one dollar each! You won't find a better deal anywhere else!"

5   A young boy stopped in front of the table. He picked up a large red stone that had flecks of crystal in it. Max had found the stone in the yard of his neighbor, Sandy.

6   "How much for this one?" the little boy asked.

7   "All stones are one dollar, sir," Max said.

8   Just then, Sandy walked out of her house. She began to walk over to Max. She looked like she was in a hurry.

9   "Maxwell Riggins," Sandy shouted, "I want half the money you make this morning!"

10   Max was shocked. He apologized to the little boy. He asked if the boy would wait just a moment. Then he turned to Sandy.

11   "Hi, there, Sandy," Max said as he forced himself to smile. "What can I do for you?"

12   "You can make me your partner," Sandy yelled. "Or you can give me back the rocks that you stole from my yard."

13   "Stole?" Max said calmly. "I didn't steal anything from you."

14   "At least ten of these rocks were on my property. You took them. It isn't right for you to make money from something that is mine."

15   The little boy put the red stone back on the table. Max began to worry. Sandy was going to make him lose a customer.

16   "Let's think about this, Sandy. I collected the rocks and I polished them. I set up the stand to sell them, too. You haven't done any of those things."

17   Sandy shook her head. She didn't care. She thought what Max was doing was the same as stealing, and she was fuming.

18   "Fine," Max finally said. "I'll give you a quarter for each stone I sell."

19   "Fifty cents," Sandy returned.

20   "That's not fair," Max told her without raising his voice. "You're right that the stones were in your yard, and I'm sorry I took them without asking you. But I did all the work. A quarter per stone is a good offer."

21   For a moment, Sandy was quiet. She realized that Max had a point. She also recalled how Max had always been honest with her in the past. She nodded and held out her hand. Max took it.

22   "It's a deal, partner," Sandy said.

LITERATURE & COMPREHENSION

11. Which describes this story's narrator?
   - **A.** This story has a first-person narrator.
   - **B.** This story has a third-person narrator.
   - **C.** This story has no narrator.
   - **D.** This story has many narrators.

12. What do readers learn in this story that they would not learn if Max was the narrator?
   - **A.** that Sandy is Max's neighbor
   - **B.** how Max feels about his stones
   - **C.** that Sandy remembers Max's honesty
   - **D.** what actions the little boy does

13. The story says that Max "admired his work," that he "smiled as he looked at the stones," and that he looks forward to being "rewarded for his hard work." Which conclusion can be drawn from this information?

    A. Max is older than Sandy.

    B. Max did not really collect the stones.

    C. Max has a great sense of humor.

    D. Max is proud of himself.

14. How would Sandy most likely react if Max refused to share any of the money he made with her?

    A. Sandy would become uninterested.

    B. Sandy would get even angrier.

    C. Sandy would grow worried.

    D. Sandy would be thrilled.

15. Which is a line of dialogue from the story?

    A. "You can make me your partner."

    B. For a moment, Sandy was quiet.

    C. He apologized to the little boy.

    D. He asked if the boy would wait just a moment.

16. What is the setting of this story?

    A. Max's backyard in the afternoon

    B. the front yard of Sandy's house at night

    C. a small room in Max's house on a rainy day

    D. a sidewalk on a sunny morning

17. Which is one of Max's character traits?

    A. He is quick to lose his temper.

    B. He is fair.

    C. He is very competitive.

    D. He is selfish.

LITERATURE & COMPREHENSION

18. How are Max and Sandy different?

   A. Max is tall and Sandy is short.

   B. Max is young and Sandy is old.

   C. Max is honest and Sandy is a liar.

   D. Max is calm and Sandy is not.

19. What makes Max worry that he is going to lose a customer?

   A. He sees the little boy put the red stone back on the table.

   B. He makes an offer to share some of the money he makes with Sandy.

   C. The little boy asks how much the red stone costs.

   D. Sandy shakes his hand and calls him her "partner."

20. What is the theme of this story?

   A. The customer is always right.

   B. Some problems have no solution.

   C. Treat others fairly and they will be reasonable.

   D. Even good people try to cheat others.

Part 4. Summarize a Fiction Passage

Write a summary of the story you read in Part 3.

.–23. Write a summary of "Sandy's Share" in your own words. Remember to use order words and describe main events from the beginning, middle, and end of the passage in your summary. Write in complete sentences and check your work for errors when you are finished. Use as much space as you need.

_____

_____

_____

_____

_____

_____

_____

_____

_____

_____

_____

_____

_____

_____

_____

LITERATURE &
COMPREHENSION

Unit Checkpoint Learning Coach Instructions
Critical Skills Practice 5

Explain to students that they are going to show what they have learned about reading and answering questions about nonfiction passages, poetry, and fiction passages, and about writing a compare-and-contrast paragraph.

1. Give students the Unit Checkpoint pages.

2. Read the directions together.

3. Use the Answer Key to score the Checkpoint, and then enter the results online.

4. Review each exercise with students. Work with students to correct any exercise that they missed.

Part 1: Nonfiction Passages

Have students read "Learn to Swim" and answer the questions.

Part 2: Poetry

Have students read "Rain in Summer" and answer the questions.

Part 3: Paired Passages

Have students read "The Danger of Earthquakes" and "Deadly Hurricanes" and answer the questions.

Part 4: Fiction Passages

Have students read "The Metal Menace" and answer the questions.

Part 5: Write a Compare-and-Contrast Paragraph

Have students write a paragraph that compares and contrasts "Talking Turkey" and "In the Woods."

Unit Checkpoint
Critical Skills Practice 5

Part 1. Nonfiction Passages
Read the passage and answer the questions.

Learn to Swim

1   When summer comes and the weather gets hot, lots of people like to swim. They jump into pools and wade in the ocean to cool off. But there is more to swimming than just splashing around. Learning to swim, even in deep water, has a lot of benefits.

2   One of the benefits of learning to swim is better safety. Many people do not like to go into water where they cannot stand. Sometimes there are accidents, though. You may not plan it, but you could end up in deep water when you least expect it. Knowing how to swim could save your life.

3   Another benefit of learning to swim is better health. Swimming is a great form of exercise. Many people swim to lose weight. It increases your muscle tone. It helps your heart and lungs get stronger. Swimming can also help your brain. People who swim are more relaxed and think more clearly.

4   Learning to swim can also build your confidence. Some people are afraid of the water. When they learn to swim, they realize that staying afloat in the water is not so hard. It helps them feel proud and strong and sure of themselves.

5   Swimming is also a fun social activity. Many pools have swim teams and lessons where you can make friends and meet new people.

6   Everyone should learn to swim. It's a fun form of exercise that you can do your whole life. Whether you just want to be safe or you want to get some exercise, learn how to swim. You will be happy that you did.

1. Why did the author write this passage?
   A. to teach readers a lesson about the dangers of swimming
   B. to make readers laugh with funny stories about swimming
   C. to convince readers that learning to swim is a good idea
   D. to explain to readers that swimming can make them smarter

2. Which sentence expresses the main idea of Paragraph 3?
   A. Many people swim to lose weight.
   B. Swimming can also help your brain.
   C. Swimming helps your heart and lungs get stronger.
   D. Another benefit of learning to swim is better health.

3. What details support the main idea of Paragraph 2?

   A. Lots of people like to swim.

   B. Some people do not like deep water.

   C. Knowing how to swim could save your life.

   D. Another benefit of learning to swim is better health.

4. Which answer best states the author's main idea in this passage?

   A. Swimming can be good for your health.

   B. Everyone should learn how to swim.

   C. Playing sports is good exercise and fun.

   D. Sometimes there are accidents around water.

5. What conclusion can be drawn after reading this passage?

   A. The author swims and enjoys it.

   B. There are few pools near the author.

   C. More pools need to teach swim lessons.

   D. People who swim are happier than other people.

Part 2. Poetry
Read the poem and answer the questions.

Rain in Summer

by Henry Wadsworth Longfellow

How beautiful is the rain!
After the dust and heat,
In the broad and fiery street,
In the narrow lane,
How beautiful is the rain!

How it clatters along the roofs,
Like the tramp of hoofs!
How it gushes and struggles out
From the throat of the overflowing spout!

Across the window pane
It pours and pours;
And swift and wide,
With a muddy tide,
Like a river down the gutter roars
The rain, the welcome rain!

6. What is the rhyme scheme of the first stanza of this poem?
   A. ABBAA
   B. ABBCC
   C. AABBC
   D. ABABA

7. Who is the speaker in this poem?
   A. Henry Wadsworth Longfellow
   B. someone watching the rain
   C. a first-person narrator
   D. a summer raincloud

8. Which line contains an example of figurative language?
   A. In the broad and fiery street,
   B. How beautiful is the rain!
   C. With a muddy tide,
   D. Like a river down the gutter roars

9. What kind of figurative language is in these lines?

   > How it clatters along the roofs,
   > Like the tramp of hoofs!

   A. onomatopoeia
   B. hyperbole
   C. simile
   D. metaphor

10. Which best states the theme of this poem?
    A. Rain is good, but it can cause a lot of damage.
    B. Rain is wonderful, especially in the summer.
    C. Rain can cause huge, muddy rivers of water.
    D. Rain sounds like a herd of horses running on the roof.

Part 3. Paired Passages
Read the two passages and answer the questions.

The Danger of Earthquakes

Earthquakes are a deadly force in nature. They can happen at almost any time and anywhere. They can destroy cities and towns. And we never know when they will strike.

Scientists know what causes earthquakes. Underneath the top layer of the earth are plates. These plates are like giant puzzle pieces. They are always moving and sliding against each other. Sometimes the plates get stuck. When they come loose, an earthquake happens.

Earthquakes do a lot of damage. They cause buildings to shake and crumble. They create huge cracks and holes in roads. They make bridges break and trees fall. Many people die every year from earthquakes.

There are ways to keep earthquakes from causing big problems. People have learned how to make buildings that will not break during an earthquake. Some buildings use stronger materials and sway when the earth moves. This keeps the buildings from falling down. These kinds of buildings should be built everywhere around the world. We never know where an earthquake will strike.

Deadly Hurricanes

Hurricanes are some of the most powerful storms on earth. They can pack winds that blow up to 200 miles per hour. They can dump gallons of rain in just minutes. Hurricanes knock down buildings and trees. They cause flooding. They can leave people without power and without homes.

A hurricane is a giant storm. It forms over the ocean. Warm and cold air meet, and water from the ocean rises. The winds begin to swirl and pick up speed. Huge rain clouds form. Then the storm moves toward land. The storm brings powerful winds, rain, and waves of ocean water.

There are things that people can do to protect themselves from hurricanes. Buildings can be built high above the ground. This protects them against the high water that comes with hurricanes. Windows can be built with a special strong glass. Then the windows are less likely to be broken in high winds. High walls can prevent sea water from flooding towns. These are some steps that people should take wherever hurricanes may strike.

11. Which problem do both of these texts discuss?

A. how to predict the next disaster

B. how to make better tracking tools

C. how to make buildings safer

D. how to stop these events from happening

12. According to these passages, which is a possible effect of both a hurricane and an earthquake?

A. They can knock down buildings.

B. They can cause flooding.

C. They can create holes in roads.

D. They can make the ground shake.

13. How are these two texts similar?

A. They predict where the next event will happen.

B. They describe the damage from these natural events.

C. They explain what people should do in an emergency.

D. They tell interesting stories about famous disasters.

14. Which generalization can be made about both of these texts?

A. All natural disasters cause people to die.

B. No one should ever live where there are hurricanes.

C. Most earthquakes can be predicted.

D. Some events in nature can cause great harm.

15. What is the opinion of both authors about natural disasters?

A. People should not live where natural disasters occur.

B. People should build strong buildings where natural disasters occur.

C. There is nothing that anyone can do about natural disasters.

D. Scientists should worry about other problems on earth besides natural disasters.

The Metal Menace

I didn't know what to do. There seemed to be no stopping the giant robot. Where had this thing come from anyway? One minute everything in Milton was peaceful. The next minute people were running for their lives.

I didn't believe the robot existed when Mayor Dan first called me. Then I saw it for myself. It was as big as a skyscraper. And now the metal monster was heading straight for the city.

My superpowers were useless against the giant. I tried blasting it with my laser. The rays just bounced off the metal skin like drops of rain. The robot was smashing everything in sight. It pulled up trees like they were daisies. Every time it took a step it left a huge crater in the road. If it got to Milton, buildings would be crushed. People would be lost.

Just then my radio buzzed. "Marshall, are you there? What's happening?" It was Tracy, my partner. Tracy and I had been friends a long time. She took care of the business end of things. I took care of fighting crime.

"Yes, I'm here," I yelled into the radio.
"Nothing seems to work against this thing! My
laser is useless. And I don't want to fly too close.
It has a mean left jab!"

"Where are you now? Where is it heading?"
Tracy asked in a worried voice.

"It's heading right for the city. It's close to the
stadium," I answered. And then it hit me. The
stadium—it was a perfect. "Hold on, Tracy, I
have a plan," I said.

"What? What plan? Marshall . . ." yelled
Tracy as I turned off the radio. I didn't have time
to explain. I had to move fast.

I flew to the nearest telephone pole. I blasted
a wire with my laser. The wire dropped to the
ground. I swooped down and picked up the end
of the wire. Then I flew in quick, tight circles
around the robot's feet. I held the end of the
wire with all my strength and waited.

Just as I had hoped, the robot's feet got
tangled in the wire. It swayed for a second. Then
it dropped to the ground with an earth-shaking
smash—right in the stadium parking lot. The fall
knocked out the robot's computer. It was over.

I took a deep breath. Good thing there wasn't
a game today!

16. Why do the rays from Marshall's laser bounce off the robot?
    A. Marshall's laser is not working correctly.
    B. Marshall does not take good aim at the robot.
    C. The robot blocks the rays with its arms.
    D. The robot's skin is made of tough metal.

17. What sequence of events is correct?
    A. The robot heads toward Milton; Marshall shoots the robot; Mayor Dan calls.
    B. Tracy calls; Marshall cuts a telephone wire; the robot falls.
    C. The robot pulls up trees; the robot nears the stadium; Marshall meets Tracy.
    D. The robot trips; Marshall shoots the robot; the robot smashes things.

18. Which character trait does Marshall have?
    A. helplessness
    B. fearfulness
    C. cleverness
    D. anger

19. How would the story be different if Tracy had told it?
    A. We would know where the robot came from.
    B. We would know what Mayor Dan was thinking.
    C. We would not know how Tracy felt about Marshall.
    D. We would not know how Marshall stopped the robot.

20. Why did the author write this story?
    A. to entertain readers with an exciting tale
    B. to inform readers about the dangers of science
    C. to show how to fight a robot
    D. to give his opinion about whether robots are real

Part 5. Write a Compare-and-Contrast Paragraph
Read the passages and then write your response.

Talking Turkey

At Thanksgiving, many people have turkey for dinner. The turkeys you eat come from farms. They have cousins who don't live on farms, though. Those are wild turkeys.

Wild turkeys have been in America for hundreds of years. The Native Americans ate them and used their feathers. The Pilgrims decided that turkeys would make good farm animals. That is how we ended up with turkeys on our dinner tables!

Wild turkeys can be found in much of the United States. They make their homes in woodlands. They look for food on the forest floor. Wild turkeys like to eat nuts, seeds, fruits, and insects. Sometimes they even eat salamanders!

Most people know turkeys by the big, red skin that hangs under their necks. This is called a wattle. It is found only on males. Male turkeys are also the only ones with big tail feathers. They fan these out to show off to the female turkeys. Wild turkeys can weigh between

5 and 18 pounds. Their wings can stretch almost 5 feet across!

The wild turkey is part of our country's history. Benjamin Franklin liked the turkey. He once said it would make a better national bird than the eagle. Maybe you think a turkey would look funny as our national symbol. But the wild turkey is a true American bird!

In the Woods

The ground crunched under Ming's feet. All around her birds twittered and chirped. Ming loved taking hikes with her father. It gave them time alone together. Sometimes they walked in silence. Other times they talked about things they saw in the woods.

On this day the trail was covered in shadows. It was early fall, so the trees still had all their leaves. Ming's father was walking in front as he always did. Ming was watching her feet. She didn't want to trip on any branches or rocks.

Suddenly Ming bumped into the back of her father. He had stopped walking. He turned around and looked down at her quietly. He had one finger pressed to his lips. Then he gently pulled Ming down behind a fallen tree.

"Do you see it?" Ming's father whispered in her ear. He was pointing over the tree trunk to a place down the trail. "It's a wild turkey."

Ming looked ahead. At first she didn't see anything. Then she saw movement. It was a large, round bird. Its feathers were a dark brown. Under the bird's chin was a pale red flap of skin. The bird had a funny, jerky way of walking. Every now and then it poked its head down at the ground.

"It's a boy turkey," said Ming's father. "See the red skin on its neck? That's a wattle. Only boy turkeys have that. He's looking for food on the ground."

Ming stared. She had never seen a live turkey before. She had only seen the ones her mother cooked at Thanksgiving. "I didn't know turkeys lived in the woods," Mind said.

"Only the wild ones do. The kinds of turkeys we eat come from farms. The Native Americans used to hunt wild turkeys. Some people still do today."

Ming and her father watched the turkey for a while until it moved away. Then they rose and continued on their walk. Ming hoped the turkey would find what he was looking for.

21.–23. Describe at least two ways that these passages are similar and at least two ways they are different. Use details from both texts to support your answer.

_____

_____

_____

_____

_____

_____

_____

_____

_____

_____

_____

_____

_____

Semester Checkpoint Learning Coach Instructions Respond in Writing

Explain that students are going to show what they have learned about comparing and contrasting reading selections.

1. Give students the Semester Checkpoint pages.

2. Read the directions together.

3. Use the Answer Key to score the Checkpoint and the Semester Checkpoint Assessment Checklist to evaluate students' response to Questions 20–25. Then enter the results online.

4. Review each exercise with students. Work with students to correct any exercise they missed.

Part 1: "The Story of Prometheus"

Have students read the passage and answer the questions.

Part 2: "What Is Fire?"

Have students read the passage and answer the questions.

Part 3: "Fire"

Have students read the poem and answer the questions.

Part 4: Respond in Writing

Have students write a paragraph comparing and contrasting two of the three checkpoint passages.

LITERATURE & COMPREHENSION

Semester Checkpoint
Respond in Writing

Part 1. "The Story of Prometheus"
Read the passage and answer the questions.

The Story of Prometheus

The Greek god Prometheus made human beings. He created men and women out of river clay. He made them look like the gods and goddesses. But Prometheus was worried about his creations. They did not have fur like animals. Animals had all the best qualities. They could run, jump, swim, see, hear, and smell better than humans. Prometheus felt that humans needed something to help protect them.

Prometheus went to Zeus, the king of the gods. He asked Zeus if he could give sacred fire to humans. Fire would help them stay warm. It would protect them from wild creatures and cook their meat. Zeus said no. Fire was a sacred power of the gods and could never be shared.

Prometheus decided to disobey Zeus. He secretly took a burning coal from the sacred fire on Mount Olympus. He carried it down to earth and gave it to humans.

Zeus was furious. He punished Prometheus. He chained him to the top of a mountain. Every day he sent an eagle to peck at Prometheus. Overnight, Prometheus would heal. Then the next day, the eagle would come back and peck at him again.

This punishment went on for many years. Then one day, Zeus forgave Prometheus and set him free. But Zeus could not take back the fire. Humans continued to use fire to help them survive. They also used it to make sacrifices to the gods.

1. What type of writing is "The Story of Prometheus"?

   _____

2. Write a brief summary of "The Story of Prometheus."

   _____

   _____

   _____

3. What is the first problem Prometheus has in the story?

   _____

   _____

   _____

4. In what two ways does Prometheus try to solve the first problem?

_____

_____

_____

5. Why does Prometheus's solution make Zeus angry? Give two reasons.

_____

_____

6. What is the consequence of Prometheus's choice?

_____

_____

_____

_____

7. What does the story explain?

_____

_____

Part 2. "What Is Fire?"
Read the passage and answer the questions.

What Is Fire?

Fire is a powerful force of nature. Fire can be very useful to us. We use fire to cook food and to help keep us warm. Fire also helps in nature when it burns old plants and trees so new ones can grow. But fire can be extremely dangerous. It can burn down buildings and whole forests in a matter of hours. What exactly is this amazing force we call fire?

Fire is a chemical reaction. It is a mixture of three things: fuel, oxygen, and heat. This is called the fire triangle. Fuel can be almost anything, such as wood or gasoline. When the fuel is heated to a very high temperature, it releases hot gases, which we call smoke. Some of the chemicals in the smoke mix with the oxygen in the air, which causes fire.

Without all three parts of the fire triangle, you cannot have a fire. You can put out a fire by removing one of the sides of the triangle. For example, water can cool down the heat in a fire. If you cover something that is on fire, you take away the oxygen. Then the fire may be put out.

LITERATURE & COMPREHENSION

Here are some safety tips to remember if there is a fire:

- If there is a fire, get away from it as fast as you can and get help.

- If you are in a building, stay low to the ground and crawl out. Smoke rises, so there is less smoke close to the ground. You can breathe more easily.

- If your clothing catches fire, the rule is Stop, Drop, and Roll: Do not run. Stop moving. Drop to the ground. Cover your face with your hands. Roll back and forth on the ground until the flames are out.

8. What kind of writing is the passage "What Is Fire?"

_____

9. What does the diagram show?

_____

_____

_____

10. What is the main idea of the second paragraph in "What Is Fire?"

_____

_____

LITERATURE & COMPREHENSION

11. What are two important details that support the main idea of the second paragraph?

_____

_____

_____

_____

12. What is the author's purpose for adding the information about "Stop, Drop, and Roll" at the end of "What Is Fire?"

_____

_____

_____

_____

13. Write a brief summary of "What Is Fire?".

_____

_____

_____

_____

Part 3. "Fire"
Read the poem and answer the questions.

Fire

by Max Wilson

1   Fire! – fire! – fire! – fire! – it sets me in a craze
    To see a first-class building all ablaze;
    A burning house resembles, when I'm **nigh**,
    Some old **acquaintance** just about to die;
5   For structures that a person often sees
    Look some like human beings – same as trees.
    (There used to be some trees on my old place
    That I'd know anywhere – just by their face.)
    And when, last night, some bells began to cry,
10 And big fire-engines rushed and rattled by,
    In just three minutes down the stairs I **strode**,
    And hurried – somewhat dressed – into the road
    (Partly to help a bit, if so might be,
    And partly, I suppose, to hear and see.) . . .

nigh – near

acquaintance – a person someone knows, but is not a
    good friend

strode – walked with long, quick steps

15   I ran like sin, and reached the fire at last:

A good-sized church was going, pretty fast.

(I'd noticed it a hundred times or more,

And several times had stepped inside the door.)

The burglar flames within had prowled around

20   A long time previous to their being found,

Till they had gained such foothold and such might

They'd turned to robbers – stealing plain in sight.

The dome and spires had on them flags of red;

They soon came thundering down from overhead.

25   It looked as if **infernal** spirits came,

To take this church away, in smoke and flame!

infernal – evil

14. What is the rhyme scheme of the first six lines of the poem "Fire"?

_____

15. What is the speaker in the poem doing?

_____

16. What type of figurative language is contained in the line "I ran like sin"?

_____

17. What kind of figurative language is contained in the line "last night, some bells began to cry"?

_____

18. In the second stanza of the poem, the speaker uses an extended metaphor. How does the speaker use a metaphor to describe the flames in the church?

_____

_____

_____

19. Read this line from the poem.

The dome and spires had on them flags of red;

What kind of figurative language is this, and what two things is the speaker comparing?

_____

_____

_____

Part 4. Respond in Writing

Write a paragraph comparing and contrasting two passages.

–25. Choose two of the three passages about fire. Write a paragraph comparing and contrasting them. Include at least five sentences in your paragraph.

- First, tell the titles of both passages and tell what type of writing each one is.

- Then, tell how the passages are similar.

- Next, tell how they are different.

- Finally, tell which passage you liked better and why.

_____

_____

_____

_____

_____

_____

_____

_____

_____

Name _____ Date _____

LITERATURE & COMPREHENSION

_____
_____
_____
_____
_____
_____
_____
_____
_____
_____
_____
_____
_____
_____
_____
_____
_____
_____

Writing Skills

Unit Checkpoint Learning Coach Instructions
Critical Skills Practice 4

Explain that students are going to show what they have learned about references, author's purpose, main ideas and supporting details, and writing prompts.

1. Give students the Unit Checkpoint pages.

2. Read the directions together. Have students complete the Checkpoint on their own.

3. Use the Answer Key to score the Checkpoint and then enter the results online.

4. Review each exercise with students. Work with students to correct any exercise they missed.

Parts 1–3. References, Author's Purpose, and Main Ideas and Supporting Details

Have students spend about 15 minutes answering the questions about references, author's purpose, and main ideas and supporting details.

Part 4. Respond to a Writing Prompt

Have students respond to the writing prompt. Tell students they have 30 minutes to complete their response.

1. Direct students' attention to Part 4 of the Checkpoint and read the directions together, ensuring that students understand they are to write a response to the writing prompt.

2. Remind students that they should write their response in complete sentences, use good handwriting, and leave spaces between words so that others can read what they wrote.

3. Have students write their response to the writing prompt.

4. Use the Writing Prompt: Rubric and Sample Responses to evaluate students' finished writing. You will be looking at students' writing to evaluate the following:

   - **Purpose and Content:** The response focuses on a time when someone the student knows surprised him or her. It describes what happened, tells who was involved, and explains why the student was surprised. It contains no more than two irrelevant facts or details.

- **Structure and Organization:** The response shows some organization and evidence of planning and revising. With perhaps one exception, it describes events in chronological order. The response is at least one paragraph in length.

- **Grammar and Mechanics:** The response has been proofread, and three or four errors remain in grammar and mechanics.

5. If students' writing scored a 1 in any category, work with them to revise and proofread their work.

Unit Checkpoint
Critical Skills Practice 4

Part 1. References
Read and answer each question.

1. Which source would be best to use to find the meaning of the word *density*?
   A. atlas
   B. encyclopedia
   C. thesaurus
   D. dictionary

2. Read this sentence.

   > Jake made a <u>poor</u> decision.

   Which resource should the writer use to find a word that means almost the same thing as *poor*, but that helps tell readers that Jake's decision was very, very poor?
   A. dictionary
   B. thesaurus
   C. atlas
   D. encyclopedia

3. Carter wants to learn more about ancient Rome. Where would he find the most information on this subject?
   A. encyclopedia article on ancient Rome
   B. dictionary entry for *Rome*
   C. atlas with maps of Rome
   D. thesaurus entry for the word *ancient*

4. Janice wants to find out who the city council members are in her hometown. Which reference would give her the most information?

   A. encyclopedia entry on local government

   B. atlas with a map of the city

   C. city council's website

   D. dictionary entry for the word *council*

5. Lena is writing a report on Spain. Which reference would make it easiest for her to see which countries are near Spain?

   A. atlas

   B. dictionary

   C. thesaurus

   D. encyclopedia

Part 2. Author's Purpose
Read and answer each question.

6. Read this passage.

   > Fresh berries are great, but they can spoil and get moldy before you have a chance to eat them. Follow these helpful steps so that moldy berries become a memory.
   >
   > 1. Mix one part vinegar with ten parts water.
   > 2. Put the berries into the mixture and swirl them around.
   > 3. Drain and rinse the berries with fresh water.
   > 4. Place the berries in the refrigerator.

   Why did the author probably write this passage?

   A. to teach people a simple way to keep berries fresh

   B. to convince readers that fresh berries taste best

   C. to remind readers that vinegar has many uses

   D. to tell readers what kinds of berries to buy

WRITING SKILLS

7. Read this passage.

Clumsy might as well be Frank's middle name. He's always tripping and bumping into things. So no one was surprised when Frank did not see the water on the ground and slipped. He didn't fall though. He just flung his arms wildly to keep his balance. He shouted and groaned. His knees wobbled. His ankles buckled. He looked like an ostrich on ice skates, and he felt very silly. But he kept a smile on his face, and everyone had a good laugh.

Why did the author most likely write this passage?

A. to warn readers to be careful around Frank

B. to entertain readers with a story about a funny event

C. to convince readers that water can be dangerous

D. to teach readers how to keep their balance if they ever slip

8. Read this passage.

> If you are going to get a dog, do not go to a pet store. Instead, go to an animal shelter. At a shelter, you can adopt a dog rather than buy one. Adoption is better than buying for a couple of reasons. The most important reason is adoption saves the life of an animal. Another reason is that adopting a dog is much cheaper than buying one. So, when you want a dog, take my advice, and go to a shelter.

Which best describes why the author wrote this passage?

A. to scare readers so that they do not want to get a pet anymore

B. to persuade readers that having a pet is a major responsibility

C. to teach readers how the pet adoption process works

D. to convince readers that adopting a dog is better than buying one from a pet store

9. Read this passage.

> The 1984 Summer Olympics were held in Los Angeles, California. Carl Lewis, an American sprinter, won four gold medals. Mary Lou Retton showed off her amazing gymnastic skills. And a young Michael Jordan led the men's basketball team to a gold medal.

What is the author's main purpose in writing this passage?

A. to persuade readers that the Summer Olympics are better than the Winter Olympics

B. to entertain readers with an exciting story about an athletic event

C. to teach readers some things about the 1984 Summer Olympics

D. to convince readers that Carl Lewis was a better athlete than Michael Jordan

Part 3. Main Ideas and Supporting Details
Read and answer each question.

10. Which sentence states the main idea of this paragraph?

> *The Last Hero* is easily the best movie to come out this year. The film is full of exciting twists and thrilling turns. In addition, the actors who star in the movie are all excellent. Lastly, the movie just looks amazing. Let me tell you more!

  A. *The Last Hero* is easily the best movie to come out this year.

  B. The film is full of exciting twists and thrilling turns.

  C. In addition, the actors who star in the movie are all excellent.

  D. Lastly, the movie just looks amazing.

11. Based on the supporting details, which sentence states the main idea that belongs at the start of this paragraph?

> _____. Jane Gallagher plays the main character in *The Last Hero*. She may look sweet and small, but she knows how to be strong, too. Ray Wilkins plays the villain, but he shows the thoughtful side of the bad guy. Finally, six-year-old Timmy Radley steals the show with his charm. Radley will win some awards for his acting.

  A. The action keeps going until the credits roll at the end of the film.

  B. The acting in the film is great.

  C. All of my friends have toys from *The Last Hero*.

  D. The only problem with the movie is its title.

WRITING SKILLS

12. Based on the main idea, which supporting detail belongs in this paragraph?

> Of course, *The Last Hero* looks terrific. Watching it is a feast for the eyes. _____.
> The 3-D effects make it feel like you are a part of the action.

A. The colors are so bright and vivid that they almost jump off the screen.

B. Even actors with small parts are great in this movie.

C. I was shocked by the movie's surprise ending.

D. No one else in my family has seen the movie yet.

13. Which supporting detail does **not** belong in this paragraph?

> If you only see one movie this year, make it *The Last Hero*. You will see more action than you've ever seen. You will watch great actors. You will even be wowed by the beauty of the movie. You should also see *Green Yellow Red*, because that's good, too. So go get your ticket today!

A. You will see more action than you've ever seen.

B. You will watch great actors.

C. You will even be wowed by the beauty of the movie.

D. You should also see *Green Yellow Red*, because that's good, too.

Part 4. Respond to a Writing Prompt
Follow the directions to write a response to the prompt.

.–16. Read the writing prompt. Then write your response on the lines.

> Tell a story about a time when someone you know
> did something to surprise you. Write at least one
> paragraph and include details about what happened,
> who was involved, and why you were surprised.

You have **30 minutes** to complete this writing assignment. Before
you begin, write down the most important ideas you want to
include. After you have finished your response, read what you
have written. Then make changes and correct mistakes in the time
you have left.

_____

_____

_____

_____

_____

_____

_____

_____